anythink

STeGOSAURUS
WOULD NOT make a GOOD
PIRATE

by Thomas Kingsley Troupe   illustrated by Steph Calvert

PICTURE WINDOW BOOKS
a capstone imprint

RÉSUMÉ

GARY STEGO

3 Prickles Lane
Rocktown, NY 40052

LENGTH	About 23-30 feet (7-9 meters)
HEIGHT	About 9 feet (2.75 meters)
WEIGHT	6,800 pounds (3,100 kg)
EXPERIENCE IN PIRATING	It's a long story.
REFERENCE	NOT this guy →

Dinosaur Daydreams is published by
Picture Window Books, a Capstone Imprint
1710 Roe Crest Drive
North Mankato, MN 56003
www.mycapstone.com

Library of Congress Cataloging-in-Publication data
is available on the Library of Congress website.

ISBN: 978-1-5158-2129-8 (library binding)
ISBN: 978-1-5158-2133-5 (paperback)
ISBN: 978-1-5158-2141-0 (eBook PDF)

Summary: Gary the Stegosaurus wants to be a pirate.
But when he gets the chance, things do NOT work out. Getting
seasick is the least of Gary's worries once he's on that ship!

Image Credit: Capstone: Jon Hughes, 23

Editor: CHRISTIANNE JONES
Designer: ASHLEE SUKER
Illustrator: STEPH CALVERT

Printed and bound in the USA.
010853S18

Ahoy, mateys! I'm **GARY** Stegosaurus. I was just fired from my pirate job, but it wasn't my fault.

For starters, Captain One-Tooth had me wear pirate clothes. I tried on hats, boots, puffy shirts, and an eye patch. But these items do **NOT** come in my size.

WARDROBE

I try to stay fit, but stegosaurs weigh a lot.
I swear it's all **MUSCLE!** No matter
where I stood, the ship nearly tipped over.

Captain One-Tooth wanted me to help raise the sails. Sounds easy, right? Well, my prickly tail shredded those sails like lettuce. I hope one of my pirate pals knows how to sew!

Even though I'm pretty big, I'm not very tall. Because
my head hangs low, I couldn't see the great ocean view.
So I climbed up to the crow's nest. I broke it, of course.
But shouldn't the main mast be a little stronger?

I needed to go to the bathroom, so I headed to the poop deck. Luckily, my pirate pals stopped me before I got started. Apparently the poop deck is **NOT** a bathroom. That would've been embarrassing!

Ye olde POOPDECK
Ye olde GALLEY

At dinner the other pirates ordered salted beef and fish. **GROSS!** I got the stink-eye when I ordered a salad. I guess they've never had dinner with an herbivore before.

After dinner we spotted another pirate ship. The guys on board were not friendly! I hit the deck to avoid getting hit by cannonballs, but my plates are hard to hide. My pirate mates were not impressed.

THE STINKY MERMAID

Thankfully, our pirate crew won the battle and plundered their treasure. Captain One-Tooth wanted me to count the gold coins, but it was tricky! What number comes after four?

When we got to shore, the pirates didn't want me to stick around. But that's okay. I'm going to start a new job as a **BRAIN SURGEON!** After all, how hard could it be?

DINO DIG

The answer to each question below is hidden in the art. Each answer is one word or number. Dig through the story until you find the answer. Good luck!

1. The stegosaurus could swing its spiky tail like a weapon. What is the arrangement of spikes on the tail called?? (page 9)

2. The stegosaurus was an herbivore, an animal that only eats plants (like moss, ferns, and low-hanging fruits). But the stegosaurus ate something else too. What was it? (page 14)

3. About how much did a stegosaurus weigh (in pounds)? (page 7)

4. About how tall was the stegosaurus (in feet)? (page 18)

5. The stegosaurus had plates on its back. Dinosaur experts think the plates controlled what? (page 17)

ANSWER KEY: 1. thagomizer 2. rocks 3. 6,800 pounds 4. 9 feet 5. temperature

MORE STEGOSAURUS FACTS

» The name *stegosaurus* means "roofed" or "covered lizard."

» Scientists don't think the stegosaurus was very smart. It had a small brain, shaped like a bent hot dog.

» Most stegosaurus bones have been found in Asia and North America. The first ones were discovered in Colorado in 1877.

» Fewer than 24 stegosaurus skeletons have been found.

» Stegosaurs lived during the late Jurassic period. That was 145 to 150 million years ago!

DINO DISCUSSION

1. Would you rather be a pirate or a dinosaur? Why?

2. What characteristics made Gary the Stegosaurus a bad pirate?

3. What job do you think a stegosaurus should have? Why?

DINO GLOSSARY

herbivore - an animal that only eats plants

plates – flat, hard pieces that cover the body of some animals

prickly – sharp

thagomizer – the arrangement of spikes on a dinosaur's tail

PIRATE GLOSSARY

crow's nest – a platform on a ship's mast used to see things that are far away

deck – the main floor of a boat or ship

mast – a tall pole that supports the sails of a boat or ship

plundered – stole things by force

poop deck – the flat surface on the raised part at the back of a ship